Robin's
Simple Recipe
For Finding A Job!

Robin L. Rask

authorHOUSE™

1663 LIBERTY DRIVE, SUITE 200
BLOOMINGTON, INDIANA 47403
(800) 839-8640
WWW.AUTHORHOUSE.COM

AuthorHouse™
1663 Liberty Drive, Suite 200
Bloomington, IN 47403
www.authorhouse.com
Phone: 1-800-839-8640

AuthorHouse™ UK Ltd.
500 Avebury Boulevard
Central Milton Keynes, MK9 2BE
www.authorhouse.co.uk
Phone: 08001974150

First published by AuthorHouse 6/23/2006

ISBN: 1-4208-7917-0 (sc)

Printed in the United States of America
Bloomington, Indiana

This book is printed on acid-free paper.

TABLE OF CONTENTS

ACKNOWLEDGEMENTS

I believe that God led me to write this book. Therefore, I want to give credit where credit is due. I want to thank San Bernardino County Superintendent of Schools for employing me to help students & adults become employed. In the process, it has helped me to grow, assist others and master my craft.

I want to thank Carol Rask, my ex-sister in law / Work Experience Coordinator who led me into the field of job developing. I want to thank Laurie Ann Snow, Recruitment/Placement Specialist & R.O.P. Instructor for helping me design the Time Management chart and all the other assistance you have and continue to provide for me. I want to thank Lindsey Mercer, Nicole King, Sarah Moretz & other staff members who helped me to prepare for all my employment workshops. You always made me look good! Therefore, this has also helped me to use some of the materials for this book. I know you all learned some new skills in the process, which will help you and others in the future.

I want to thank my many friends and family members for all their love, patience and support. Especially, since many times I am not available for fun and socialization due to many obligations and responsibilities. I also want to thank my ministry partners who have and continuously give me strength and encouragement through their daily messages.

Especially, since demonic forces try so hard to keep me from doing what God wants me to do. I have made so much Lemonade that I could open a Business. This could be another topic for a future book! For those of you who do not know what this means. When life deals you Lemon's you make Lemonade.

Last but surely not least, a big thank you to Author House. I could not have done this without you! Your staff is nothing short of courteous and dedicated. It seems no matter where I go there is always someone who needs a job and someone who is asking me, who is hiring and what advice can I offer? As long as the Earth remains there will always be someone who needs a job! Therefore, I believe this book is Timeless!

I dedicate this book To All of You, who may be seeking employment or know someone who needs a job! Good luck to all of you and God Bless!

> **"Do not go where the path may lead, go instead where there is no path and leave a trail."**
> *- Ralph Waldo Emerson*

In all thy ways acknowledge him, and he shall direct thy path.
Proverbs 3:6

ROBIN'S INGREDIENTS FOR FINDING A JOB

1. Steps to Finding A Job
Looking for a job is much like going on a diet. If you stick to the plan
it will work if you do not then it will not. The key to finding a job is
to follow the recipe steps, be persistent and follow up.

2. R.O.P. & Free Training
Regional Occupational programs are available in most High Schools.
There are classes with training for almost every field you desire.

3. David's Story
This is a story of how my son obtained a job by following my recipe for
finding a job.

4. Tools for Finding A Job
A few simple necessities you will need to begin your job search, such as
the right clothes, a resumé, sample application etc.

5. Application Process
Anytime you apply for a job you always need to have a sample application filled out to take with you. Applications may be a way to screen
you out if you do not have them filled out completely and neatly.

6. The Job Search

Always dress to interview, know where you are going, be prepared to interview, go alone and take a job search log with you. It is vital that you write down where you went, the date, the manager's name and what they said. Therefore, you will be able to follow up.

7. Job Shadowing & Informational Interviews

The best way to find out about a job or a career in which you are interested in is to talk to the people who are actually doing that job or talk to people who hire those people. It is also a foot in the door for obtaining a job in the future.

8. Resumés

A resumé is a brief summary of your qualifications and where you have worked. It is an essential tool for all job seekers and must be updated every time there is a change. There are five components that must be on all resumés regardless of which format you choose. It should always be ready to apply for your next job.

9. Interviews

There are different types of interviews, the importance of interviewing is being able to talk about yourself and sell yourself to the employer. You need to be prepared, look and act as if you want the job. It will take practice and rehearsing in front of the mirror. An interview is also a two way process.

10. Portfolios

Another tool to assist you in obtaining a job. A portfolio is a notebook of your accomplishments, awards, references, your resumé and recommendation letters. Kind of like your brag book. Which you should take to your interviews. Once you have one started, you just keep adding to it.

11. Attitude & Self-Esteem

Having a positive attitude and being motivated are crucial in the success of obtaining a job or anything else you pursue. Some people have low self-esteem of themselves, which affects their confidence in obtaining employment. Especially if it takes longer then they anticipated. This is where we have to accept who we are and learn to do the best we can with what we have.

12. Time Management

Many people make excuses for not being able to find a job, including that they are too busy and do not have the time to search. You have to schedule time to look for work just as you do with anything else. We all have 24 hours in a day and seven days in a week, how you spend your time is up to you.

RESOURCES ENCLOSED

- Sources of Employment
- Tips for Participating in Job Fairs
- Questions and Answers about R.O.P.
- Military Training Programs
- How to Dress for the Interview
- Sample Application
- Personal Reference sheet
- Job Search Log
- How to conduct an Informational Interview
- Resumé Outline & Examples
- Resumé Key Phrases & Action word list
- Sample of Job Objectives
- Sample Cover Letter
- List of sample Interview Questions
- Questions you may want to Ask
- Personal Strengths
- If you are offered the job & how to keep your Job
- Example Letter of Resignation
- Why People May Not Get Hired
- What to include in a Portfolio
- Sample Letter of Recommendation
- Renewing your mind with Affirmations
- Self-Esteem

- Time Management Chart
- Time Management Flyer
- 14 Steps to Success
- Robin's Simple Recipe For Finding a Job!

Chapter One

STEPS TO FINDING A JOB!

Looking for work can be one of the hardest jobs you will ever have. Once you have a job, it will be easier to get another job. I have a saying about getting a job, looking for a job is much like going on a diet. We all know if we stick to the plan, we will loose the weight if not, we wont. It is that simple! Even when you go on a diet, you have to first make a decision to do so. Then you have to plan your shopping for your meals and stick to the eating program until you loose the weight, which may also include exercise, which many of us hate. Diets work much faster and better if we include at least three days of exercise. You do not have to join a gym to exercise, you can find simple exercises to do at home while watching TV or get involved in your favorite sport such as playing tennis. You will be doing something you love and get in shape at the same time. The problem with many of us is that when we do not see quick results we tend to give up. Keep in mind that persistency is the key to all victory no matter what you do, including finding a job.

I have been a job developer for over 17 years and have worked with hundreds of students and adults teaching them how to find a job and actually putting them to work through direct hires and various programs. The ones that are serious about going to work follow my simple recipe and go to work. The ones that are not serious or motivated do not. Many students and adults come to me looking for jobs, I explain to them what they need to do and give them all kinds of resources verbal and tangible, and then they get disappointed because they actually have to do the leg work. Many people just expect others to hand them a job. In the real world, it does not usually work that way.

I believe that anyone who wants a job bad enough will have one. God created us all to do something and to be someone; he did not intend for us to be lazy. Our bodies are designed for movement. God also put gifts and talents into each of us; even people with disabilities who want to work do so. We just need to find out what our gifts and talents are. Some of us are blessed to be singers, artists, etc. Sometimes we know shortly after birth and sometimes it may take years to find out.

I believe we all have a call and purpose in our life. It took me many years and going through many jobs to find out what I enjoy and what I am good at. My first job was in retail, which is a good place for a teenager to start. Only God knows what else you and I can accomplish while we remain on this Earth.

Think about what you like to do, what you can do, and or what you are good at and then seek a job in that area. You may have to get into some training programs, volunteer, go to school, job shadow or go through several jobs before you find your true calling. Also, keep in mind that each job is a stepping-stone to another job. With each job you gain experience and responsibility.

THE KEY IS TO GET STARTED!

Most people do not start work until they are sixteen due to having to obtain a work permit. Some people come to me and say, "Robin no – one will hire me because I do not have any experience." That is true with some companies; it also depends on the job. If you dress appropriately, show enthusiasm and can answer some simple questions about yourself and have a true desire to work then employers will give you a chance. I will be sharing all the tools you will need shortly. Some situations due depend on your age.

Looking for a job is a job like anything else you pursue. You may want to tell everyone you know that you are looking for a job. You never know, your next door neighbor could be an employer or own a business. My son found that out at one point.

- The Job Corps hires men and women ages 16-24 years of age.

- The California Conservation Corps (C.C.C.) hires men and women ages 18-23 years of age. The training you receive in these programs will open more opportunities for future employment.

- Apprenticeship Programs have many trades available with good pay.

- Schools & Colleges have a variety of programs that can put you to work.

- Job Fairs are a great way to find employment opportunities.

- Job Hotlines are avenues to find employment. Most schools, Hospitals, Cities, Utility Companies and Counties will have one.

- Web Sites are also very common for finding employment. Many businesses advertise their jobs online. There are also many businesses who take applications regularly and or hire often. Some even have regular scheduled days where they conduct interviews.

There are many resources and opportunities available so make sure to research your possibilities.

"All Dreams can come true if we have the courage to pursue them."
-Walt Disney

The Job Search

You need to find specific openings in your chosen area(s) of interest. Check:

Newspapers	Placement/ Employment Agencies
Trade magazines, professional associations, magazines and newsletters. Read the classified/help wanted ads. (Avoid ads for get rich quick schemes.) Sundays are the best!	And job-hunting services. They'll help you find a job for a fee. In some cases, the employer will pay this fee for the person who's hired. (Check out agencies thoroughly before signing a contract for services.)
Schools	**Bulletin Boards**
Including vocational training centers, high schools and college. Ask the school counselor for job listing. (Most job services are limited to students and alumni of the school.)	In post offices, libraries, union offices and personnel offices in corporate and government buildings.
Government Offices	**Your Contacts**
Such as local employment or human resources offices. They may have listings available jobs or they may direct you to other helpful agencies. Some agencies offer free job counseling, placement and referral.	Research Job Fairs C.C.C. Job Corp Military Apprenticeships R.O.P.

At this stage you must clarify what you're looking for:
- Full-time employment
- Part-time or temporary work
- Free-lance or work-at-home jobs
- Summer / vacation-time-jobs
- Or... do you want to start your own business?

An Informational Interview

Finding out about a company you may want to work for.

Call and request an appointment to talk about requirements in the field you've chosen (state that you are only seeking information) Ask for someone in personnel, the manager or owner of the company.

Sources of Employment

- Apprenticeship Programs
- Business Directories
- California Conservation Corps (C.C.C.)
- Canvassing
- Chamber of Commerce
- Civil Service Announcements
- Communications Media
- Employment Development Department
- Industrial Parks
- Job Bulletin Boards
- Job Corps
- Job Fairs
- Local Newspapers
- Manufacturers or Distributors of Special Equipment Used at Work
- Military Services
- Newspaper Advertisements
- Prior Employers & Employers to Whom Applications are Made
- Private Employment Agencies
- Professional & Business Associations
- Radio, TV, Newspapers & Magazine Stories of New or Expanding Companies or Areas
- R.O.P. Job training
- School Placement Services
- Suppliers, Customers & Competitors of Prior Employers
- Teachers, Religious Advisors, Insurance Agents, Creditors, Bankers
- Trade Associations & Trade Publications
- Unions...Friends, Relatives & Neighbors
- Web sites, monster.com
- Yellow Pages

"A GOOD PERCENTAGE OF JOBS ARE FILLED THRU NETWORKING"

Tips for Participating in Job Fairs

1. Dress professionally- Wear a suit if possible. Handle this as you would a regular interview. Always dress to impress!

2. Wear comfortable shoes- lines are frequently long and you should expect to wait, especially for some of the popular companies. Bring a sample application with you that is already filled out, so you can just transfer the information.

3. Resumés- Bring a supply of resumés to hand out to the companies.

4. Take a portfolio/briefcase to hold resumés and corporate literature.

5. Prepare a "one-minute commercial"- Think about your strong points, your goals, the company, and where you want to go within the company.

6. Be prepared to discuss where you want to work geographically. What you like doing, what you're looking for in a job and what your most relevant skills are.

7. Arrive early- Plan on extra time for checking in.

8. Network- While you are waiting in line, talk to others. You may hear about opportunities of which you were unaware.

9. Be assertive and show initiative – shake hands and introduce yourself to the employers and recruiters when you reach the table.

10. Be enthusiastic- Employer surveys identify the single most important personal attribute applicants can bring to their first

regular employment position is enthusiasm. So, smile and project interest in the company.

11. There will be many applicants approaching employers at the same time you are…DON'T BE OVERWHELMED by the experience. Keep a positive attitude and concentrate on the benefits of the experience.

12. Explore options- A wide variety of companies will normally participate. This is an excellent opportunity to browse and indulge your curiosity.

13. Make sure to write down what companies you applied at and whom you spoke to. Then later you can make your follow-up calls. Get business cards if available.

You do not have a second chance to make a first impression!

CHAPTER TWO

R.O.P. & FREE TRAINING

If you are at least sixteen you, can go to any of the high schools and enroll in R.O.P., which stands for Regional Occupational Program. That is the only requirement for R.O.P. and it is FREE! It is also an awesome program for adults. There are classes for almost every type of career you want to pursue it can also be a stepping-stone or an alternative to college.

Just to name a few of the classes, there are several types of Medical classes, Nursing, Banking, Office Occupations, Law Enforcement, Child care, Teacher Assistant, Dental Assisting, Cosmetology, Restaurant Occupations, Welding, Graphic Arts, TV production and the list goes on. Some of the classes actually put you to work so you can get hands on experience in that job. Once you complete the class, you will get a certificate. If you are still in school, you will get high school credits as well. Teachers will teach you employment skills and there is usually a job developer for each school who can help you with employment and other resources.

I also teach an R.O.P. class in the evenings called Diversified Occupations. The class is 180 hours, 80 hours are spent in the classroom, and 100 hours are spent on a job site of your choice. Example, if one of my students wants to be an attorney, I will place them into a law office to get experience. If the student does well and the employer has an opening, they are usually hired. If there are no openings, students are encouraged to check back often, because R.O.P. is a foot in the door. In addition, you will have something else to put on your application and Resumé. And many get hired as a result of taking R.O.P.

Check with your local High School District regarding R.O.P. classes, which are open to those that are from 16-106 years of age! (..) Depending on where you live, there may be an alternative name for R.O.P.

"It is never too late to be what you might have been".

-George Ernst

Questions and Answers about R.O.P.

HISTORY

The San Bernardino County Superintendent of Schools Regional Occupational Program was organized in 1973 by the County Superintendent's Office and a group of ten participating school districts. The SBCSS R.O.P. is accredited by the Western Association of Schools and Colleges (WASC).

What Is The Purpose Of The Regional Occupational Program?

The R.O.P. provides open entry, open exit career technical education and support services that augment and expand the capabilities of our school districts. Our courses provide instruction for entry-level employment, advanced training, and upgrading skills. R.O.P. courses are limited to occupational areas where there is reasonable expectation of employment or postsecondary articulation, and where there is sufficient student interest.

How Many Districts Are Served By The SBCSS R.O.P.?

There are currently sixteen secondary districts:

Apple Valley • Baker Valley • Barstow • Bear Valley

Fontana • Hesperia • Lucerne Valley • Morongo

Needles • Rialto • Rim of the World • San Bernardino City

Silver Valley • Snowline • Trona • Victor Valley

Two other ROPs serve the following county school districts:

Colton, Redlands, Yucaipa - CRYROP (909) 793-3115

www.cryrop.k12.ca.us

Chaffey, Chino Valley, Claremont, Upland -

Baldy View R.O.P.
(909) 624-0063 www.
baldyviewrop.com

HOW IS THE R.O.P. ADMINISTERED?

The San Bernardino County Superintendent of Schools employs a director and staff to oversee the budget, develop instructional programs and to provide support services within R.O.P. operational guidelines. The San Bernardino County Superintendent of Schools R.O.P. is organized on a decentralized basis contracting with districts to run individual programs that meet local student and employer needs. Each district manages the day-to-day operation of the courses they offer. Our governance structure consists of a Board of Directors made up of the County Superintendent of Schools and the superintendents of the sixteen member districts and Coordi-nating Council, an advisory body composed of district representatives.

How Is The R.O.P. Funded?

The R.O.P. has an average enrollment of 14,000 with a base Average Daily Attendance (ADA) of 2,238. Apportionment funds (ADA) are received from the state to finance its operations. Each program is designed to be self-supporting based on funding received from student hourly attendance. Lottery dollars are also allocated based on ADA and used to purchase new equipment and materials. No federal funds are included in the R.O.P. operational revenues.

This R.O.P. does not charge tuition; however, students may be required to purchase certain materials and books which they can keep. Unless specifically noted otherwise, students will be responsible for providing their own transportation to class locations including community classroom sites.

Who Attends R.O.P. Classes?

Depending on the policies of the member district, any high school student over 16 or adult may attend an R.O.P. class offered in any district served by our R.O.P.. To maintain the original concept of R.O.P., high school students receive priority in enrolling in any class; however, adults are welcome on a space-available basis. Travel distance is the only limitation on inter-district attendance.

Who Are The R.O.P. Instructors?

R.O.P. instructors are specialists from business and industry chosen for their expertise and experience in their particular subject field. Each instructor is credentialed by the California Teaching Commission and is required to complete designated teaching methodology classes.

Where Are The R.O.P. Classes Offered?

R.O.P. classes are offered either on local campuses and/or in local businesses where potential employment actually exists. Community facilities and equipment are utilized under formal agreements signed by the business representative and the County Superintendent of Schools to provide a combination of school site and work site learning.

When Are R.O.P. Classes Offered?

Most R.O.P. classes are offered during the day to meet the needs of high school students, adults and our participating businesses. Some classes are offered in the evening to accommodate working adults.

Can School Credit Be Earned For Taking R.O.P. Classes?

High school students who satisfactorily complete the course requirements can be granted credit according to local district policies. R.O.P. students completing a course receive a Certificate of Competency, which is signed by the instructor. In addition, many classes are articulated with local community colleges.

What Is Meant By Articulated Classes?

Articulation is an agreement between the R.O.P. and community colleges or four-year colleges which allows a student to receive some type of credit towards a college course for competencies learned in the R.O.P. courses.

Does The R.O.P. Offer Guidance And Counseling Services?

The San Bernardino County Superintendent of Schools R.O.P. offers a variety of services to potential and enrolled R.O.P. students. These support services include career and educational counseling, career assessment, career planning assistance, educational and occupational information and job search placement assistance.

Are Employers Involved With The R.O.P.?

Employers support the R.O.P. in a variety of ways. Through their participation on advisory committees, business leaders assist in verifying local labor market demand, determining curriculum content, providing expert consultants and recommending qualified instructors. In addition, employers provide facilities, equipment, and promote student job placement.

Printed by permission

Military Training Programs

Some students may need the guidance and discipline that the various branches of the armed forces can provide.

TECHNICAL SCHOOLS   The military technical schools are considered among the best in the world. They combine on-the-job training with excellent professional instruction. Many high school graduates are opting to develop skills in career fields of the future, rather than to attend college right away. Technical schools offer a good start for the career-building process. Experienced trainers in every job area provide practical, personalized training. And it is put to use right away in a job in the armed forces.

APPRENTICESHIP PROGRAMS   Some skills can lead to certification of completion of apprenticeship in jobs comparable to civilian fields trades in apprentice program include: carpenter, cement mason, commercial photographer, cook, machinist, maintenance mechanic, and power plant operator.

ENLISTED PROGRAMS   The armed forces is one of the largest employers and finest teachers of young people today. Men and women are assured of expert training for jobs matched to their abilities and interests in many skilled fields. For almost every job advertised in your local paper, there is a similar job in the armed forces.

The variety of jobs in the Armed Forces offer interesting work to suit all temperaments: outdoor or indoor; do-it-yourself; student; adventurer; and the person who seeks challenge and early leadership responsibilities. There's a place for all of them in the Armed Forces if they qualify.

Whatever skill field you chose, all Armed Forces personnel enjoy the same pay and promotion schedules, and great benefits unequaled in the civilian workforce. Among those benefits are:

- 30 days of paid vacation every year
- advanced education at little or no cost
- excellent retirement program after only 20 years of service
- extra pay for certain types of duty
- free housing and meals
- free medical and dental care
- free or low-cost entertainment facilities, including gyms, movies, bowling alleys, lounges, golf courses, and campgrounds
- full pay and allowances during training
- regular promotions based on ability
- savings from shopping at military stores

In short, the Armed Forces gives young people a solid foundation for the future.

Printed by permission, Partners & Education/Youth Programs/Poway Unified School District

CHAPTER THREE

DAVID'S STORY

My son David took my R.O.P. evening class when he was 15 ½ on a waiver. Permit me to share the outcome with you. He sat in the back of the room and I am sure he thought that it is just my Mom up there preaching again. What does she know? I had originally placed him in a retail store for his training phase. He did well but was not formally hired cause the employer lacked openings at the time. This happens. The employer told him to keep checking back and that she would hire him as soon as there was an opening. Well, David took her advice and kept checking back. She even made him fill out another application. After several weeks he became very discouraged, feeling that the employer gave him the run-around. I told him sometimes that also happens. I suggested that he never risk everything on one endeavor, as I tell all my job seekers. "The more places you go to apply for a job, and keep going back, the sooner you will get hired." At that time David was not serious about looking for a job. He just kept going back to that one place because the employer said she would hire him.

Before David ever took the R.O.P. training or was old enough to be employed he worked around the neighborhood and washing cars and doing yard work. Later he got some experience in construction and setting tile. He even discovered a neighbor of ours who had a business and he would work for him when he needed help. After taking the R.O.P. class, David put together his resum'e with all that experience.

When he finally decided he was ready to go to work because I would not keep giving him money, I reminded him of what I taught him in the class. " Oh, Mom, "he said," I do not want to do all that to get a job." I responded, " Well, then, my son, you do not want a job badly enough." He also told me he did not know what he wanted to do with his life; yet. So, I said to him, "You need to just get off your behind, find a job, and eventually you will figure out what you want to do. Just get started! At least you will have money in your pocket while you are figuring it out." He thought about it and then we went shopping for interview clothes. I strongly encourage parents to invest some extra time & money in their kids if they want them to succeed in their job search. If there are not funds for suitable interview clothes, then borrow them or try thrift stores.

Once David had his clothes, we made several copies of his resum'e; placed them in a folder with his sample application to take with him and an erasable pen. Then I drove him to various prospective employers. He then went inside got the application filled it out and turned it in. Yes, this took time. A couple of weeks, to be exact. The main key to getting a job is persistence. Go back to where you applied and remind the employer that you are still interested. This is where many applicants fail. Like so many others, my son hated looking for a job because it took too long. I encouraged him to keep it up until he receives an offer. I also reminded him to pray, have faith and a positive attitude. His efforts did pay off after a few weeks and he landed a job in a grocery store. After six months, he moved out of state to live with his dad. His dad told him if he wanted to live with him, he had to go to work. This time however, David had to walk to look for work. Now I know people do not particularly want to do that. Fortunately, his dad lived in an apartment in Las Vegas, and there were businesses close by. He remembered what I taught him about getting a job and much to my surprise; he was hired at the first place he applied. Why? Because he was prepared. He was dressed to interview, brought a proper resum'e, took his sample application so he could copy his information to their form with his erasable pen. He also had white-out just in case. He shook the employers hand with confidence, smiled, and was able to be his own advocate during the interview. Eventually he left that job and got two other jobs afterwards even though he had to walk in the rain at night to and from work. It was also much further.

He came back to live with me again after he graduated from High School. I told him, he will need to pay me rent and for use of the car. I gave him a resource list of prospective employers who accept applications on a regular basis and routinely hire. At one company he interviewed on the spot, took a math test, and was asked to return in a few days for a drug test. He did and was hired full time! Unfortunately, my son, being a bit immature as some kids are at that age decided not to go to work one day. Nor, did he call his employer, so it was an automatic loss of his job. I believe he learned a valuable lesson. It gave me an opportunity to stress that every job is a stepping-stone to another. I said, " Be careful not to burn bridges along the way because you need to have good employment references."

I also reminded him once again that it often takes two incomes in a family to pay for bills and a few extras along the way. I think after the years he has seen how hard I had to work and that it often takes two jobs for a single parent to have what we had. So two weeks later, he said "I will get a job at XYC Company," and he did! After awhile we talked about his future and how he will support himself in an entry-level retail job. It is very difficult for young high school graduates to work in retail or minimum wage jobs and live completely on their own. Most have to find roommates or two jobs.

My parents and I had discussed with him the array of benefits the military could provide. At first, this path did not interest him. We asked him, " Where else can you go and have an immediate job, roof over your head, free food, a salary, free training, traveling prospects and structure all at the same time?" I am proud to say he is now serving in the U.S. Air Force. From someone who seldom made his bed while he was at home; he was named " the master bed maker" in his flight.

My son told me that one of the best things that I ever taught him was how to find a job. He even told his friends to listen to my advice. I may be forgiven for saying it warmed my heart. My son was very stubborn and we had many challenges. I know, if he can do it so can you!

An old Chinese Proverb says, "Give a man a fish and you feed him for a day. Teach a man to fish and you feed him for a lifetime." Think about the wisdom in this! I truly believe in this when it comes to teaching people how to find a job. By using my strategy and ingredients for finding a job, "I am confident you will be able to obtain a job each time."

Be wary of giving up somewhere in the middle. Remember, nothing changes on the outside till you make a decision on the inside. So, if you are really serious and motivated to find a job, please read on. There is a job waiting for you!

    * " **True Life is lived when tiny changes occur.**"

-Leo Tolstoy

Chapter Four

TOOLS FOR FINDING A JOB & CLOTHING ATTIRE

TOOLS YOU NEED TO FIND A JOB:

1. Dress clothes & shoes
2. Sample Application
3. Resumé
4. A folder to put sample application in, and several resumés
5. Able to answer questions about yourself
6. Possible portfolio to show accomplishments
7. Knowing where to apply for a job
8. Resources / Networking
9. Figuring out your transportation
10. Having child care available for those who need it
11. Blue or Black pen
12. White out or erasable pen
13. Motivation, a positive attitude and determination

At the end of this book, I will have a short, simple, step- by- step procedure that you may be able to tear out or to review to make it simple.

Now that you have all that, I will get you started on your job search and your future job.

STEP ONE / Clothing Attire

Get interview clothes, you always want to dress to impress whether you are going out to look for a job or on an interview. You do not have a second chance to make a first impression. If you are a male, you need to have a nice pair of dress pants with a button down dress shirt and tie. Also, need to have nice dress shoes. Whatever color pants you wear, try, and wear, the same color socks. Females, should always wear a dress or skirt. If not, a nice pantsuit will work. Make sure not to have long dangly earrings or over done hair and makeup. In addition, ladies, do not wear open-toed shoes. Never show your midriff or cleavage unless you are applying for a modeling job. Whether you are a male or female you should not display any visible tattoos or earrings other than being on your ears. Guys, when applying for a job, if you have an earring, take it off. The dress code when applying for a job should be no different than when you dress to go on an interview. In fact, when you look for a job, always be dressed to interview and prepared, because you can be interviewed right then and there and walk away with a job. This happens often.

Dress for Success

Winning Appearance

Conservative

Simple

Neat and Clean

Matching Colors

In Good Taste

Nothing "Trendy"

Nothing "Flashy"

How to Dress for your Job Interview

Attire- Men

Appropriate	Inappropriate
• Dress Shirt/ Button Down	• T- Shirts
• Pressed Slacks	• Blue Jeans
• Dress Shoes	• Shorts
• Dark Socks	• Tennis Shoes
• Tie (If Appropriate)	• Gym/ Exercise Clothes
• Sports Coat	• Heavy Cologne or Aftershave
• Suit (Professional)	• Earrings Visible Tattoos
	• Facial Piercing (Tongue, Nose)

Attire- Woman

Appropriate	Inappropriate
• Skirt	• Mini Skirts/ Shorts
• Blouse	• T-Shirts
• Dress	• Tight Dresses
• Suit (Dark Colors)	• Blue Jeans
• Blazer/ Jacket	• Gym/ Exercise Clothes
• Nylons (Skin Tones)	• Heavy Makeup/ Perfume
• Dress Shoes (Pumps, Low Heels)	• Bright Nail Polish
• Simple Jewelry	• See-through Clothing
	• Visible Tattoos
	• Facial Piercing (Tongue, Nose)

CHAPTER FIVE

APPLICATION PROCEDURE

STEP TWO / Application Process

Get yourself an application from any company and fill it out. This will be your sample application that you put in a folder and take with you when you apply for jobs. This way, you will have all the information with you. Such as places you worked with employers names, phone numbers, addresses, dates when you started and when you left, your salary and reason you left. Applications usually ask for two to three references with people's names, their occupations and phone numbers. Applications ask for where you went to school etc. You want to always make sure, when you go to a business to apply for a job, that you have all the necessary information with you so look prepared. There are places that do not let you take the application home so you will need to fill it out right there. When you fill out an application, it may srceen you right out of a job if you do not have all the information filled out.

The first thing an employer looks for when they look at your application is to make sure it is complete and neat. If there is a question that does not apply to you, do not leave it blank. Any time you leave a question blank; they will assume you forgot it. Make sure you always put something in the space. If it does not apply, write N/A, which stands for Not Applicable. Alternatively, put a dash or write none.

The next thing an employer usually looks for is your availability. When are you available to go to work? Students who are in school usually fail in this section because they write open or anytime. If you are in school, you need to write down the times you are available to actually work. If you are available on the weekends, then put open or anytime. You may be the right person for the job but if the employer is looking to hire someone for the morning shift and you are in school then he cannot hire you.

When the application asks for salary desired put open or negotiable, unless you know what the starting salary is. Why would you put minimum wage for salary desired if the company will pay you much more? It helps to research a company before you apply; then you will know the salary and expectations. I will explain how you can do that as well when we cover informational interviews in chapter seven.

Applications ask for position desired, do not put open unless you are willing to take anything including scrubbing bathrooms. Find out what the positions are. If you are applying at a Restaurant, do you want to be a busboy, dishwasher, waitress, or manager? If you really do not know, then put entry-level. You will usually start at the bottom and then work your way up. Always make sure you sign and date your application. It also helps if you have someone else look at your application to review it before you turn it in. More eyes are usually better than one.

I referred a student to an employer who thought her application looked great and she even had someone else look at it. I did not hear from her for a while so I checked with the employer to see if he had a chance to review her application. Thank God, I called the employer, he said, "Yes, her application looks great, but I can not call her in because she did not sign it." I immediately called her and she went to sign the application, was then interviewed and hired.

Many applicants make the mistake of filling out applications in pencil and sometimes in pink or green ink thinking that their application will stand out and be reviewed right away. They are right, they do stand out and are placed in the round file, and then the applicants sit by the phone wondering when the employer is going to call. They will be waiting and wondering for a long time.

When you submit your application, it may also help to attach your resum'e to the application with a paperclip. Again, you never know, you may be interviewed as soon as you turn it in.

COMPUTER / APPLICATION DESK

Many companies now use computers for you to apply for a position and then give an employment test afterwards. This can take anywhere from one to two hours. Many people do not get hired cause they cannot pass the tests. Please read the questions carefully, most of them are common sense. However, some are a bit tricky. Once you have filled your application out online make sure to contact the store manager or someone in personnel to let them know. Otherwise, they may never call you, especially if you seemed to be the right person for the job but did not pass the test.

If you are applying online make sure to have all your employment information with you. There are also companies that will allow you to apply online right from home.

"Your future depends on many things, but mostly on you."
-Frank Tyger

MASTER APPLICATION
PLEASE PRINT CLEARLY AND ANSWER ALL QUESTIONS FULLY

Date of Application:_____

NAME_____

LAST   FIRST   MIDDLE

ADDRESS_____

CITY_____STATE_____ZIP_____PHONE(_____)_____

SOCIAL SECURITY NUMBER_____-____-_____   (Optional)

Do you have a Class C (Regular) Driver's License?   ☐ Yes   ☐ No   California ID?   ☐ Yes   ☐ No

Schedule Desired: ☐ Full Time   ☐ Part Time   ☐ Seasonal   Date Available for work _____

Shift Desired: ☐ Day   ☐ Evenings   ☐ Any Hours   Salary Expected: $_____

		Sunday	Monday	Tuesday	Wednesday	Thursday	Friday	Saturday
Available	Day							
Hours	Evening							

List activities or commitments that may interfere with attendance requirements:_____
_____

POSITION APPLYING FOR:_____ Are you 18 years old or older?   ☐ Yes   ☐ No

Do you have any relatives employed by this company?   ☐ Yes   ☐ No

Are you eligible/authorized to work in the United States?   ☐ Yes   ☐ No

WORK HISTORY: List ALL employment beginning with the most recent. Include military, voluntary and unpaid work experience.

Company	Period of Employment & Salary	Title & Description
Supervisor	From: To:	
Phone ( )	Start:$ End:$	
Address		
City/State/Zip		
Reason for Leaving		
Company	Period of Employment & Salary	Title & Description
Supervisor	From: To:	
Phone ( )	Start:$ End:$	
Address		
City/State/Zip		
Reason for Leaving		
Company	Period of Employment & Salary	Title & Description
Supervisor	From: To:	
Phone ( )	Start:$ End:$	
Address		
City/State/Zip		
Reason for Leaving		
Company	Period of Employment & Salary	Title & Description
Supervisor	From: To:	
Phone ( )	Start:$ End:$	
Address		
City/State/Zip		
Reason for Leaving		

(OVER PLEASE)

Company	Period of Employment & Salary	Title & Description
Supervisor	From: To:	
Phone ( )	Start:$ End:$	
Address		
City/State/Zip		
Reason for Leaving		
Company	Period of Employment & Salary	Title & Description
Supervisor	From: To:	
Phone ( )	Start:$ End:$	
Address		
City/State/Zip		
Reason for Leaving		

What method of transportation will you use?_____

Can you speak any foreign languages?_____

Have you ever been convicted of a felony? ☐ Yes ☐ No If yes, please explain_____

A conviction may not neccesarily bar you from employment. Each conviction will be judged on its own merits with respect to time, circumstances and seriousness.

Can you pass a drug test **TODAY**? ☐ Yes ☐ No   If no, Please explain:_____

Describe any special training or skills you have:_____

Additional Information for Placement Consideration_____

Education

	School Name	Location	Graduate	Degree	Major/Minor	G.P.A.
High School						
College						
Business/Tech						
Other / ROP						

References

Name	Address, City, State & Phone	Business	Years Known

I certify that all the information submitted by me on this application is true and complete to the best of my knowledge.

Date_____ Signature_____

Personal References

Be prepared for your job search by lining-up at least three (3) personal references. A person that knows you well, and will speak highly of your character gives a personal reference. Do not list relatives as personal references.

List three (3) personal references below. It is VERY IMPORTANT that you get permission from the individuals listed to use their names as references.

1.

_____   _____
NAME   **TELEPHONE NUMBER**

_____   _____
ADDRESS   **OCCUPATION**

_____   _____
CITY, STATE, ZIP   **YEARS KNOWN BY YOU**

2.

_____   _____
NAME   **TELEPHONE NUMBER**

_____   _____
ADDRESS   **OCCUPATION**

_____   _____
CITY, STATE, ZIP   **YEARS KNOWN BY YOU**

3.

_____   _____
NAME   **TELEPHONE NUMBER**

_____   _____
ADDRESS   **OCCUPATION**

_____   _____
CITY, STATE, ZIP   **YEARS KNOWN BY YOU**

CHAPTER SIX

THE JOB SEARCH

STEP THREE / The Job Search

When applying for a job, make sure you always go alone. If your only way of getting there is for someone to take you, then make sure you leave him or her outside.

I was in a clothing store in the mall one day talking to a manager about how applicants dress etc. when they apply for a job. Then in walked three ladies together, probably in their late thirties, and asked for an application. The manager and I both looked at each other and smiled. She told them she was all out. After they left, we laughed because they came in a group to apply. Later as I was walking in the mall, I saw the three ladies together again. I couldn't help myself, so I went up to them and very kindly said, "excuse me, I was in that clothing store speaking with the manager when the three of you came in together to ask for an application." They just looked at me somewhat strange, I said, " Can I give you a tip?" They agreed" I asked if they were all looking for a job and they said, yes. Then I said, " The next place you go to apply, go alone." " They said ok, we did not know." I saw them again later at different times and they were all alone.

About a week later, I was in the mall again talking to another manager and she had shown me a stack of applications, some of them in pencil, some in different colored ink and some very sloppy. In walked a young lady with shorts on, tennis shoes and her belly showing, she asked if she could have an application. The employer said, "Sorry, we are all out come back tomorrow." The employer and I were thinking that she had no clue. The employer really was out of applications. I ran into this girl in the mall again. She was sitting down, and I walked up to her and greeted her. You came into the store where I was meeting with the manager to ask for an application and she told you to come back tomorrow because she was out of applications. Can I make a suggestion to you when you go back? If you are serious about getting a job, no offence but do not dress like that when you apply for a job. When you go in tomorrow, dress up. Whenever you are out and you see a help wanted sign somewhere, please look at yourself are you ready to walk in and apply for a job? Do you have all your information with you? If, not go home, change and bring all the information with you that you will need to fill out the application.

Prior to being pregnant, I was in public relations. After I gave birth to my son, I wanted to stay home until he was about six months old. I was married at the time and my husband definitely wanted me to work and so did I. I was cranky when I was unemployed. I want to have my own money. I did not want to be the kind of wife that has to say, "Honey can I have some money to buy something?" Therefore, in order to stay home and still have money, I started a day care. I was able to take care of my son and make money at the same time. I then got two part time jobs, one in the evenings and one on weekends. Which allowed us to save money to go on vacation.

After six months I had enough of kids and the two part time jobs. I was ready to go back to work at one job. I was shopping at a grocery store one Saturday afternoon and when I walked into the store, I noticed a Help Wanted sign in the window. Are you wondering what I did? I did my shopping, went home, and put my groceries away. Then I changed clothes, gathered my resum'e and sample application, and drove back to the store. I went in asked for an application sat in my car and filled it out. Then I walked in and asked for the manager by name. He recognized me as a regular customer. I gave him the application and resum'e; he took me upstairs, interviewed me, and hired me on the spot. Why? Because, I was prepared.

Once you have your clothing chosen, and a sample application, also make sure you put a resumé together. You will need a folder and a pen to take with you. You will need a tablet or a "job leads log" so that you can keep track of where you go, when you went, who the manager was and what was said, so that you can do your follow-up. The key to finding a job is persistence and follow-up. There is a log sheet included where you can keep track of where you go.

Next, you should have an idea of where you want to work so you will know where to go. For instance if you want to work in a restaurant, be specific. Do you want fast food or a nice restaurant? Then decide which ones, write them down and apply at those restaurants. Never go to just one or two places, the more places you go to, the sooner you will obtain your job. I always recommend that you start with five to ten places. So, choose your 10 restaurants and then figure out how you will get to them. Do you have your own transportation? If so, great, if not, who will take you? Maybe a friend, a parent, or by using a bicycle, walking, or taking the bus. Example; you start off by going to the Red Robin, go inside, walk up to the counter or hostess desk, and ask whom you can see to receive a job application. Once you get it, sit somewhere and fill it out. Once it is all filled out, you take it back in and ask to see the manager. If you were smart and planned ahead you could have called in advance to find out who the manager is so when you get ready to turn your application in you would know who to ask for. Example, the manager comes out, what do you do? You extend your hand for a handshake with a smile, and say your name. Example, "Hello Mr. Jones, my name is Robin Rask, I just wanted to give you my application and let you know that I am really interested in working here." That is all you have to say. He will do the rest. Now this can go several ways. He can say, "Sorry we are not hiring right now, but we will keep your application on file." This is where people get discouraged. He may say, "We will be hiring next month, feel free to check back, or call me Tuesday at 4:00." Or he may look at you and your application and then start asking you some questions and depending on what he hears and sees, you may be offered a job at that time or be asked to come back. Now if he says, "Call me Tuesday at 4:00" and you do not, you have just told him that you do not want the job. That is why it is so important to write down where you go and what is said to you. When Tuesday comes and it is 4:00, you can simply pick up the phone and call the Red Robin. This is what you say, "Hello, is Mr. Jones in?" Mr. Jones comes on the phone, and then you say, "Hi Mr. Jones, I am Robin Rask. I dropped off my application to you last week and you told me to call you today at this time, I am still interested in working for you." Again, he will take it from there. You did exactly what he told you to do. If Mr. Jones told you that they are not hiring right now, that is ok. You write that down and go see him again next week or the following. He may just tell you to come in for an interview. Someone is hiring every day; just because they do not have a job opening today does not mean they won't tomorrow, next week or next month. Someone is always leaving a job somewhere. People either quit, take maternity leave, are promoted, move, are let go or are fired.

My suggestion to you is to go to ten places, get your applications in, and meet the managers. Then every week to every two weeks go back to all those ten places dressed up and ask for the manager again. Re-introduce yourself, example, "Hi, Mr. Jones, I am Robin Rask. I was in two weeks ago to drop off my application and want to let you know I am really interested in working here at the Red Robin." Again, listen to what he says and write it down. He may still not be hiring. By the third time you visit an employer and introduce yourself again, he will recognize you. You may have to do this several times with each company you apply for before you obtain the job.

Do not get discouraged, do not give up and stay determined and persistent. Let us say you have done this consistently with ten employers for three months and still you are unemployed. It could happen, and if it does, stop and ask yourself what you are doing or not doing. If you feel you are doing everything right and still those places are not hiring, then find out if there are more businesses in your town. Chances are there are hundreds. That is what I mean about not risking everything on one endeavor. Seek ten more businesses and do exactly the same thing and you can still follow up on the others. Eventually this will pay off. You may have to apply at a place you do not really care for. However, it will give you experience, money and on your days off you can continue to look for what you really want. There may also be times when you go to apply at a business and they are out of applications, this is then the time to give them your resumé and ask when they will have more applications so you can come back.

Remember it is easier to find a job once you have one. Keep in mind, that God answers prayers; he knows your wants and needs. " The ones who search the most are the ones who find the most." -ASW

When you are looking for a job, there are many resources available. Learn to talk to people, find out what agencies are in your town that help people find jobs. You can even find jobs online. There should be no excuses for not obtaining a job if you really need one and are able to work. If you need help, it is out there. As Joyce Myers says, "Excuses are just reasons stuffed in a lie."

"There is no man living who is not capable of doing more than he thinks he can do."

-Henry Ford

Job Search Contacts

Date	Employer Name & Address	Phone Number & Contact Person	Currently Hiring	Date Contacted	Comments/Notes
		Phone Number: Contact Person: Title:	___Yes___No When___	Follow-up:	Application Submitted:__Yes__No When___ Resumé Submitted:___Yes___No When___ Interview Scheduled:___Yes___No When___
		Phone Number: Contact Person: Title:	___Yes___No When___	Follow-up:	Application Submitted:__Yes__No When___ Resumé Submitted:___Yes___No When___ Interview Scheduled:___Yes___No When___
		Phone Number: Contact Person: Title:	___Yes___No When___	Follow-up:	Application Submitted:__Yes__No When___ Resumé Submitted:___Yes___No When___ Interview Scheduled:___Yes___No When___

Chapter Seven

JOB SHADOWING AND INFORMATIONAL INTERVIEWS

STEP FOUR / Job Shadowing & Informational Interviews

If you are not sure of what you want to do or you think you might want to do something but do not know what it takes to do that job or get into that field, you can follow someone around and watch them. This is called," Job Shadowing." One of my students thought she wanted to cut hair but was not sure. Instead of referring her to Beauty School or R.O.P. first, I called a salon to see if she can come in for a few days, observe, and ask questions. She did this for three days and decided that was not what she wanted to do. I remember when I was younger and thought I wanted to work with animals, I volunteered at an animal hospital for a few weeks. I love animals, but did not like to see them die. I soon discovered that was not the job for me, however it was great experience.

INFORMATIONAL INTERVIEWS

The best way to find out about a job or a career area in which you are interested in is to talk to the people who are actually doing the job or talk to the people who hire those people. Informational interviewing is a foot in the door and an extremely effective tool for finding a job and or deciding what you want to do and do not want to do. You could actually make a career out of this. An informational interview is not applying for a job; it is strictly obtaining information about a specific job or career. Therefore, it is not as nerve-wracking. Think of it as if you were a journalist doing a story. In other words, you are the one asking the questions. This can be fun and informative at the same time. It may also help you to gain more confidence. I tell my applicants this is a golden method, but most people do not want to go to all this trouble. Again, those who search the most, find the most. God says the same thing, "seek and you shall find."

You may be reading this and thinking, I thought she was going to give me simple steps to obtaining a job, I did not realize I had to read all this, have all this and do all this. You will see the whole process summarized at the end. And to what is involved in finding a job, the resources, other ways to obtain a job, and why some people are not successful in obtaining a job. Trust me, once you read and then apply the steps, you will obtain a job, unless you really do not want one. I am being positive for you while you are reading this. With this information and God on your side, you cannot lose.

CONDUCTING YOUR
INFORMATIONAL INTERVIEW

Choose a job you would like or a career you want to pursue. You can do this with any company you want. Let us say you want to work for Best Buy. Pick up the phone, call Best Buy and ask the manager's name. Thank them and hang up. Ok, now write down some questions that you might want to know about Best Buy and how to get a job there. Then call Best Buy and set up a time where you can meet with the manager and ask him or her those questions. Your intent will be now to set up a meeting to find out about the company. When you are ready, call Best Buy ask for the manager. When the manager comes on the phone say, "Hi Mr. Smith my name is Robin and I am doing some research and was wondering if I could set up an informational interview with you at your convenience to find out about your company." Mr. Smith might say sure, and then you set up a time and date. Now remember, you are not going on a job interview, you are only gathering information. However, in the back of your mind you want to work for Best Buy but you cannot tell them that.

You need to come up with five or six questions. For example, What are the different types of positions you have here and what are their duties, how did Best Buy get started, how many stores do you have and where are some of their locations, how often do you hire, what is your method of hiring, what do you look for in an applicant, what is your entry-level salary, what are your expectations, what is your dress code, does your company offer promotions, do you provide training, etc. You come up with the questions. Write your questions down on a tablet, take them with you, and leave enough room to write your answers. If you are the type of person who has difficulties writing down the information and listening at the same time, take a tape recorder with you. At the meeting, make sure you ask the employer if it is ok to tape the conversation.

When you go to this informational interview, it is extremely important that you dress to impress. Therefore, dress the way you would go to apply for a job and be professional. Some, of you may be uncomfortable doing this but this will help get you use to dressing professionally especially if you do this with more than one employer. This may also boost your confidence. When you go, make sure you are on time. It is always best to be early. When you walk in ask for Mr. Smith. Mr. Smith comes out, shake his hand, and greet him by saying," Hello Mr. Smith, I am Robin, I spoke to you on the phone about meeting with you today to discuss your company." Chances are you will go into his office and sit down.

Before you get started, it is important for you to break the ice first before going into all your questions. Please do not forget this! You can start by saying, " great office," or "looks like you are busy here today." This may help if you are a bit nervous. Once you sit down, your first question should always be about the employer. Always ask something of them first such as, how long have you been working for Best Buy, do you enjoy your job? That is your icebreaker, and then when the time is right you go into all your questions. This interview could take anywhere from 15 minutes to an hour depending on their time. At the end of that interview, make sure you thank them for their time, shake their hand again and ask for a business card. There are times that when you conduct this interview the employer could say, well we are hiring right now why don't you pick up an application on your way out. What would you say? I bet most of you would say sure and take an application. Wrong, do not do that! When you do, then you will have tricked the employer and lied to them. Your intent was to obtain information not apply for a job. You say well then what am I supposed to do? You simply say, well thank you but I just came to interview you and get some information, I am not prepared to apply for a job today, and may I think about this? You go home, sleep on it, and come back later when you have all your information with you to apply for the job. Now, if the employer insists that you take the application then do so.

Remember in the back of your mind you are interested in this job or career field. So, ask questions that will help you to find out what the employer is looking for when they hire. Or what kind of experience is needed in the field. This will help you to prepare, especially if you need to attend college.

When you arrive home, put a thank you card or letter in the mail to thank them personally for their valuable time. Then evaluate the meeting, does this sound like a company you want to work for or not? If not, go somewhere else and do exactly the same thing. If it does, then go back later and apply for a job. The employer already knows who you are and will admire you for coming in on your own time to inquire about their company.

When you go back to fill out the application, ask for Mr. Smith. You can say, "Mr. Smith after I interviewed you, I decided I would like to work here and I am here to apply for a job." The rest is in his hands.

"Continues effort – Not strength or intelligence is the key to unlocking our potential."
-Winston Churchill

Another Approach...The Informational Interview

The best way to find out about a job or career area in which you are interested is to talk to the people who are actually doing the job—or even better, talk to the person who hires those people. This method of employer contact called "the informational interview" can also be a very effective job-seeking method.

To arrange for an informational interview, call the Personnel Department of a company and ask to talk with the person who hires workers in the area of your interest. Ask if you can set up an appointment to come in and talk with him or her for about 15 minutes at their convenience. Explain that you are thinking about going into that type of work someday and would like to know more about the work as well as what kind of training, experience, and personality characteristics the employer prefers.

REMEMBER! You are *seeking information* **and** *not interviewing for a job*. **You will be asking the questions of the employer so you should be prepared. You should dress appropriately and act businesslike, as you will want to leave a positive impression with the employer. Be courteous and sensitive to the cues of the employer.**

Do not take up too much of the employer's time since they are doing you a favor by agreeing to talk with you. Most employers do not mind this type of request and feel flattered to have their advice sought.

When you have finished with your list of questions for the employer, thank him or her for their time. Do not offer a copy of your resumé. If the employer requests it, return with it at a later time. You do not want the employer to feel "tricked" into a job interview.

Sometimes, you may find out that you are already qualified for the job about which you are inquiring. An employer may request your resumé or suggest that you apply for a specific job. Employers sometimes suggest further contact and may even give you permission to use their name. These happenings would be extra benefits to your main goal of seeking "information" although some experts have speculated that doing information interviews actually more than doubles your job seeking success.

Always be courteous and try to make a good impression. You never know when you may again encounter that employer as you are applying for jobs or even once you are working on a job. Finally, be certain to send the employer a brief letter thanking him or her for taking the time to talk to you.

Dream Job Informational Interview Worksheet

Company's Name: _____   Date: _____

Interviewer's Name: _____   Phone No.: _____

Student's Name: _____

REQUIREMENT QUESTIONS
QUESTIONS & ANSWERS

	Would I like this?	Could I do this?
1. What are the job duties?	Yes No	Yes No
2. What are the training or educational requirements of the job?	Yes No	Yes No
3. What experience must people have to start here?	Yes No	Yes No
4. What are the physical demands of the job (lifting, standing, etc)?	Yes No	Yes No
5. What are the hours of the job?	Yes No	Yes No
6. What kinds of equipment (vehicles, machinery, computers, etc., must a worker be able to operate to do the job?	Yes No	Yes No
7. Are there other jobs in this field that might have fewer requirements?	Yes No	Yes No

WORK SKILLS QUESTIONS
QUESTIONS & ANSWERS

	Would I like this?		Could I do this?	
1. How important are speed and accuracy on this job?	Yes	No	Yes	No
2. What are the company's safety practices?	Yes	No	Yes	No
3. What is the daily routine of the job?	Yes	No	Yes	No
4. What are the reading, writing and math requirements of the job?	Yes	No	Yes	No

SOCIAL SKILLS QUESTIONS
QUESTIONS & ANSWERS

	Would I like this?		Could I do this?	
1. Do workers have contact with customers? If yes, what is the policy for customer interaction?	Yes	No	Yes	No
2. Does the company have a probation period?	Yes	No	Yes	No
3. Does the company have social activities?	Yes	No	Yes	No

PERSONAL SKILLS QUESTIONS
QUESTIONS & ANSWERS

	Would I like this?		Could I do this?	
1. What is the dress code?	Yes	No	Yes	No
2. What kind of personal traits must workers have to do this job?	Yes	No	Yes	No
3. What things must workers have (uniforms, lunch, special shoes, tools., etc.)?	Yes	No	Yes	No

COMPANY POLICY AND ATMOSPHERE QUESTIONS
QUESTIONS & ANSWERS

	Would I like this?		Could I do this?	
1. How often do people get hired?	Yes	No	Yes	No
2. How does the company hire – newspaper, agencies, walk-ins, referrals, EDD?	Yes	No	Yes	No
3. What is the entry level wage for this job?	Yes	No	Yes	No
4. What benefits can workers at this site receive?	Yes	No	Yes	No
5. What kind of training do workers receive?	Yes	No	Yes	No
6. Are workers closely supervised?	Yes	No	Yes	No

7. How are workers evaluated?	Yes	No	Yes	No
8. Is there a possibility of promotion?	Yes	No	Yes	No

SUMMARY

Would I like this job?   YES   NO
(Consider the number of times you chose "Yes" and "No" in the "Would I like this?" column.)

Why or why not?

Could I do this job?   YES   NO
(Consider the number of times you chose "Yes" and "No" in the "Could I do this" column.

Why or why not?

Additional questions or comments:

Resumés

STEP FIVE / Resumé

Make sure you have a resumé to show where you have worked, skills you have, and where you went to school. General rule for a resumé is to keep it to one page. For administrative positions it may be longer, depending on the amount of experience you have. Your resumé always needs to be typed with no errors. There are three types of resumés: a functional skills resumé, chronological or a combination of both. No matter what format you use on your resumé you will need to have the five components on it.

*Personal information, at the top, which is your name, physical address and phone number. Then underneath write:

- Job Objective, you can write entry-level, or name the title of the job position, or make the objective open enough to where you can use the resumé anywhere you apply. Such as, seeking an entry-level position where I can utilize my skills and abilities with a company that has opportunity for growth and advancement.

- Work Experience, list company names of places you worked at, your job title, and the duties you performed.

- Education, write The names of schools you have attended, making sure to include internships and R.O.P. You can list your G.P.A., awards, clubs, sports, being a T.A. etc.

- Skills, if you have any additional skills, list them, being bilingual is a big plus

- Extra curricular activities, whether in school or volunteer

- References available upon request, which can then be in your portfolio

Resumés are not as intimidating as they sound. If you cannot type or do not have access to a computer, then have someone do it for you or use someone's computer. You can even pay to have it done. Always make sure you have plenty of copies and never give out the last one. Every time you change jobs, get some new experience, take a new class, or change your address or phone number you will need to change and update your resumé. Your resumé should always be updated and ready to apply to your next job. If you just got a job and you have been there for a little while, update your resumé with the name of the company you are working for, your title and duties. You never know when the next opportunity will knock at your door. When I show or explain how to start putting a resumé together, I start by suggesting the person to get in front of a computer and make an outline. Enclosed is a sample of a Skills Resumé, some call it a Functional Resumé. This may be the simplest resumé you can write. It is appropriate for people with limited experience or for those who have a wide range of backgrounds and levels of experience.

Name
Address
Phone

OBJECTIVE: Seeking an entry-level position where I can utilize my skills and abilities with a company that has opportunity for advancement.

CAPABILITIES (List all the duties that you did at each of the jobs you held, including other skills and things you can do. Do not forget to write down Bilingual.

*
*
*
*
*
*

EXPERIENCE (Write name of company you worked for and job title) Include volunteer work and childcare.

*
*
*
*
*
*

EDUCATION

EXTRA CURRICULAR ACTIVITIES

REFERENCES FURNISHED UPON REQUEST

Once you have your outline, just fill in the blanks. Some of you may say, well, I have never worked before and do not have any experience.

If you are at least sixteen years of age, you have had some experiences in life. I babysat before I was of age to work, back then I made fifty cents an hour, a dollar an hour when I was lucky. You can write "child care attendant for the Jones family" on your resumé and write down what you did. Example; read stories, facilitated activities, planned meals and supervised small children.

Some of you may have been a teacher's assistant while in school. Everyone has to start out somewhere. If you are young, you may not have as much information to put on your resumé, But with time that will change. Just get started, you will have to space it out and bold your headings to make it look more like a complete page. If you are a "domestic engineer / homemaker" and have never worked outside The Home because you raise children then just focus on the skills you have obtained. Being a homemaker brings out many skills such as cooking, planning, budgeting etc.

There is also a list of action words and phrases you can use. The action words are used in place of "I". The only time "I" may be used is in the objective of the resumé.

Always use action words that describe what you have done or what you can do.

If you are sending your resumé in the mail or by fax, always make sure to include a cover letter. The cover letter needs to state to whom it is going or to whom it may concern. Please see enclosed sample.

Please refer to the resumé outline and then see what your completed resumé may look like.

"Nothing great was ever achieved without enthusiasm."
- Ralph Waldo Emerson

MARYANN NEEDY
1407 (Good Old "Hire-Me" Lane!)
Victorville, CA 92392
(760) 955-0000

OBJECTIVE: Seeking an entry-level position where I can utilize my skills and abilities with a company that has opportunity for growth and advancement.

CAPABILITIES

- In charge of inventory and customer service
- Operated cash register and collected money for fund raisers
- Greeted and seated customers
- Assisted with customer carry outs, bagged groceries, returned merchandise to shelves, swept floors, blocked merchandise and ran for customer price checks
- Delivered newspapers and collected money for customer billing
- Assisted teachers with call slips, ran errands and graded papers
- Typing and computer skills, operated copy & fax machines and set appointments
- In charge of filing documents, data entry, and taking accurate phone messages
- Supervised small children, planned meals, activities and read stories
- Bilingual, dependable, eager to learn, and a team player

EXPERIENCE

- Sales Associate at Sears
- Hostess at Marie Callenders Restaurant
- Courtesy Clerk at Stater Brothers
- Office Assistant at Desert Valley Dental
- Teacher's Assistant at Victor Valley High School
- Child Care Provider for local Neighbors

- Volunteer at the Red Cross
- Washed and waxed cars for Neighbors
- Snack Bar Attendant for the High Desert Soccer League
- News Paper Carrier for the Daily Press

EDUCATION

Victor Valley High School
Information Processing R.O.P. class
Cheer Leader, Annual Staff
G.P.A. 4.0 / Honor Roll / Perfect Attendance
Cal State San Bernardino

REFERENCES FURNISHED UPON REQUEST

Resumé Key Phrases

Key Phrases that will catch their attention. Below are some descriptive comments you may include in your resumé or application to help describe your personality, experience and abilities.

Goal Oriented

Self-Motivated

Well organized

Enjoy a Challenge

Reliable prompt

Able to learn quickly

Able to meet deadlines

Strong managerial skills

Resourceful, problem solver

Enthusiastic team member

Able to work under pressure

Take pride in a job well done

Outstanding Leadership skills

Strong sense of responsibility

Good with numbers and figures

Committed to completing a job

Excellent communication skills

Able to work well unsupervised

Able to prioritize a heavy workload

Multi task oriented

Action Words

You may find this list helpful when writing a resumé or listing your accomplishments.

- Achievement
- Acquired
- Adapted
- Addressed
- Administered
- Advised
- Analyzed
- Anticipated
- Appraised
- Arbitrated
- Arranged
- Assembled
- Assisted
- Audited
- Awarded
- Budgeted
- Built
- Calculated
- Centralized
- Changed
- Charted
- Classified
- Coached
- Collaborated
- Collected
- Compiled
- Completed

- Delegated
- Delivered
- Demonstrated
- Designed
- Detected
- Developed
- Devised
- Diagnosed
- Directed
- Discovered
- Dispensed
- Displayed
- Disproved
- Distributed
- Doubled
- Drafted
- Drew Up
- Edited
- Eliminated
- Endured
- Enforced
- Established
- Estimated
- Evaluated
- Examined
- Exhibited
- Expanded

- Inspected
- Installed
- Instituted
- Instructed
- Insured
- Interpreted
- Interviewed
- Invented
- Investigated
- Launched
- Lectured
- Listened
- Located
- Logged
- Maintained
- Managed
- Mapped
- Marketed
- Measured
- Meditated
- Minimized
- Monitored
- Motivated
- Navigated
- Negotiated
- Observed
- Obtained

- Purchased
- Questioned
- Read
- Realized
- Received
- Recommended
- Recorded
- Recruited
- Reduced
- Rehabilitated
- Reorganized
- Repaired
- Reported
- Represented
- Researched
- Resolved
- Restored
- Reviewed
- Rewrote
- Routed
- Scheduled
- Selected
- Separated
- Served
- Set Up
- Simplified
- Sketched

- Composed
- Compounded
- Conceptualized
- Condensed
- Conducted
- Confronted
- Conserved
- Constructed
- Consulted
- Contracted
- Controlled
- Converted
- Coordinated

- Corresponded

- Counseled
- Created
- Criticized
- Cultivated
- Dealt With
- Decided

- Explained
- Expressed
- Facilitated
- Forecasted
- Formed
- Formulated
- Found
- Founded
- Gathered
- Generated
- Guided
- Handled
- Handled Complaints

- Handled Detail Work

- Hired
- Identified
- Implemented
- Improved
- Informed
- Initiated

- Operated
- Organized
- Originated
- Oversaw
- Performed
- Persuaded
- Planned
- Predicted
- Prepared
- Presented
- Prevented
- Printed
- Processed

- Produced

- Promoted
- Proposed
- Protected
- Provided
- Publicized
- Published

- Sold
- Solved
- Spoke
- Staffed
- Studied
- Supervised
- Supplied
- Surveyed
- Taught
- Tested
- Timed
- Tolerated
- Trained

- Translated

- Treated
- Trouble-Shot
- Updated
- Utilized
- Worked
- Wrote

Scannable Resumé

There are a few different ways you can write your resumé, by using the chronological format, the skills format, or a combination of both. You may also choose to have your resumé scanned so you can use the scannable format. You need to decide which works best for you.

A growing number of companies are using software packages to store, track, and search the resumés they receive. Which means computers are now viewing your resumé more then humans, so you can scan your resumé online and reach more companies.

If you are getting ready to apply for a job and submit your resumé to a company and are not sure that they scan resumés then you can always call the Human Resource Department or Personnel Office first.

In place of writing out your Objective or in addition to on your resumé, you write the word KEYWORDS as a heading. Or you write it under Objective or above. Under Keywords you want to use noun skilled words that catch the search engines attention based on the skills, degrees and experience you have. You need to find out what the key words are for the job you are seeking. If there is a job posting or announcement, there may be keywords enclosed on the job description that you can use.

When you mail your resumé to a company if you have Keywords listed, they can scan it right into their database. Then if it meets the Employers needs, it will be pulled up for review and you may receive an interview. If you are not sure how to do this then ask someone for help. There are many programs and agencies that assist people in finding jobs. Here is an example of how to use the Keyword section on your resumé:

Keywords

Human Resources, Management, Organizational Skills, Administrative Assistant, Supervisor, Program Coordinator, Time Management Skills, Leader, Team Player, Honor Student, IBM, MS Word, Spreadsheet, Power Point, Desk Top Publishing, Bilingual, PHD, Willing to Relocate.

Sample Resumé
in Scannable Format

MARY ANN NEEDY
1407 Hire Me Lane
Victorville, CA 92392
(760) 955-0000
E-mail: MaryAnn@aol.com

KEYWORDS

Customer Service, Office Assistant, Time Management, Organizational Skills, Bilingual, Team Player, Computer Literate, Money Management, Trained New Employees, Willing to Train, Willing to Relocate.

OBJECTIVE

Seeking an Office Assistant position, which will utilize my computer and organizational skills and lead to increased responsibility and advancement.

EDUCATION

Cal State San Bernardino, San Bernardino California
Currently attending for Business Administration Degree
Victor Valley High School, Victorville California
R.O.P. Financial and Office Occupations classes
Computer Experience and Training: Word, Excel & Power Point
Relevant Course Work: General Office practices, Training and Development, Transactions and Computer Applications.

EXPERIENCE

Bank Of America, Victorville, CA
January 2005 to present
Bank Teller

Performed basic teller transactions, responsible for balancing cash drawer and providing quality service.

ACHIEVEMENTS / ACTIVITIES

Outstanding student of the year, Deans List, Volunteer Community Assistant, Employee of the Month, Tennis Coach.

REFERENCES FURNISHED UPON REQUEST

Resumé Writing Skills

Sample Job Objectives For Your Resumé:

Seeking an entry-level position where I can utilize, and further develop my skills and abilities with a company that has opportunity for growth and advancement.

Entry-level.

Seeking a position as a Nurse's Assistant.

To pursue a career with a progressive organization in a responsible and challenging position utilizing my experience and skills.

Seeking an entry-level customer services related position in a challenging environment that provides opportunity for advancement.

Seeking part-time or full-time employment.

Career Objective:

Professional career in the area of Administration or Public Relations with an established firm who will utilize my positive attitude, leadership abilities, and communication skills.

Energetic high school graduate with excellent communication and organizational skills pursuing a career in specialty or technical marketing.

Energetic college student with excellent communication and organizational skills pursuing a career in accounting or related position in a financial environment.

Objective Summary:

Position as an Electronics Engineering Technician. Over eight years of experience in electronics, including design, modification, and technical support of SATCOM, computer hardware/ software, communication, radar, and navigation systems. An exceptional technician consistently recognized for money saving solutions to complex technical problems.

To obtain a challenging position with a progressive company that can use my experiences and my liberal arts education.

To obtain a challenging position with a progressive company that can offer me an opportunity for advancement.

To contribute positively to the public relations effort of a dynamic company.

Summary:

A summary is a list of three to five highlights of your achievements and qualifications that should precede your work history or functional skills. The summary is a great way to grab attention and inspire the reader. Some examples:

Effective problem solver using excellent verbal written communications skills.

Excellent track record for generating overall cost for education and operation efficiency improvements.

M.B.A. from Harvard University in Business Management.

Strong leadership skills while advancing team player approach.

Successfully managed budgets in excess of $3 million.

Possess special talent for identifying client's needs and presenting effective solutions.

15 years of proven leadership abilities with an excellent record of achievement.

Aim of Resumé

The goal is to bring you to the interview stage. Stress, what you can offer, not what your looking for; accomplishments, results and solutions, not just descriptions.

Consider

Preparing several resumés, each designed for a special job or company.

Contact Your References

Get their permission before you give their names. Select references who are most appropriate for the job you're applying for.

MaryAnn Needy
1407 Hire Me Lane
Victorville, CA 92392
(760) 955-0000

Objective: To apply business skills acquired in class and during part-time employment to a full-time office position.

Experience:
    2005-Present   Bank Teller
                     Bank Of America

       Duties:
           Performed basic teller transactions, responsible for balancing cash drawer and providing quality customer service.

    2003-2005   Vons Grocery Store
                     Courtesy Clerk

       Duties:
           Trained new employees; assisted with customer carry outs & bagged groceries

Skills
    Trained in Word, Excel & Power Point
    Typing skills at 80 wpm
    Knowledge of office machines
    Fluent in Spanish.
    Excellent organizational and Time Management skills

Education
    Victor Valley High School
    Teacher Assistant
    R.O.P. Financial & Office Occupations
    Named outstanding student of the year

Personal Interests
    Chess, sailing, reading, writing and assisting others.

References: available upon request.

Sample Cover Letter

Date:

Ms. Robin Rask
Executive Vice-President and CEO
Diamond Design Industries
7777 Diamond Drive
Victorville, CA 92393

Dear Ms. Rask:

It is with interest and enthusiasm that I am applying for a position as an assistant sales representative. I have acquired excellent retail/merchandising skills in a class I recently completed offered by the County Regional Occupational Program (R.O.P.). I believe the hands-on experience I received will be of particular interest to you.

I have enclosed my resumé and a copy of my R.O.P. certificate for your review.

I have always admired the Diamond Design Industries fashion line and am confident that you can use someone with my particular background, skills, and abilities. I look forward to hearing from you regarding a personal interview.

Thank you for your time and consideration.

Sincerely,

MaryAnn Needy

MaryAnn Needy
1407 Hire Me Lane
Victorville, CA 92392
(760) 955-0000

Enclosures: Resumé, R.O.P. Certificate

CHAPTER NINE

INTERVIEWS

STEP SIX / Interviews

There are different types of interviews. Most of them one on one, some on the phone, sometimes group interviews with other applicants and sometimes panel interviews where there are several people sitting around a table interviewing you at the same time. Talk about nerve-wracking. Some interviews are short and some are lengthy. Sometimes you may be interviewed by two different people.

The number one question in an interview is usually, "Tell me about yourself." The easiest question about ourselves to answer, yet so many struggle with that response. You know yourselves better than anyone except for God so this should be your easiest answer. Employers may ask you several questions to find out about you and why they should hire you. So, be ready to talk about your strengths, weaknesses, goals, skills, and why you want to work there. Whether you interview with one person or several at the same time, always make sure you shake the employer's hand before and after the interview and smile. It is very important that you maintain eye contact with the employer and speak so they can hear you, and show enthusiasm for the job. At the end of the interview, they may ask you, "Do you have any questions you would like to ask of us?" Never say no. When you say no, you have told the interviewer that you are not that interested in the job.

Many times, they are so busy asking you questions they do not share enough of the job requirements with you. Therefore, this is your opportunity to find out more about the company, especially if you have not done any research. You should always ask what the dress code is and not to assume anything. One of my students showed up in shorts the first day of work because he did not know the dress code and was sent home to change. Here are just a few sample questions you can ask the employer. Always make sure to ask questions that show interest and enthusiasm for the job.

- What are his or her expectations of the person they want to hire for this position?
- How will my progress be evaluated once I am hired
- Do you have a probation period?
- Are there opportunities for advancement?
- Does your company provide training?
- Is there a training manual?
- When might you be making your decision or when can I start?

If you do not get the job, it is ok to call back and find out why. Otherwise, how will you know what to prepare for on your next interview? There could be several reasons why you were not hired. I went on a panel interview once for an education position that I knew I was qualified for and could do. It was similar to what I was already doing. However, it was a panel interview and I knew two of the people that I would be interviewing with, one of them I was very intimidated by so I was very nervous. I thought I did everything right and answered all their questions. However, I did not get the job and I wondered why. Therefore, I called to find out and thank God that I did. The gentleman told me I did very well and seemed very qualified but the job required more enthusiasm and I did not display that. Talk about being upset with myself. Six months later, the person that they hired did not work out and I re-applied and was very enthusiastic and got the job! Had I not asked before I would have never known!

SUGGESTIONS FOR PREPARING FOR AN INTERVIEW

Every morning when you wake up and get ready for the day, look in the mirror. Even though there are days you may not want to do this, it is great training and preparation for your interview and self-confidence.

When you are shaving, or doing your hair or make up in front of the mirror, simply talk to yourself. I know it sounds funny but it works. Say positive statements about yourself. Such as, I am responsible, friendly, outgoing, a fast learner, a team player, goal oriented, work well with others, punctual, and always take initiative. Say positive things about yourself to sell yourself in an interview. This will also boost your confidence, which everyone can use. When you are in the interview elaborate on your attributes. Many applicants tend to say, "I am a hard worker," instead you need to explain to the employer what makes you a hard worker. When you tell the employer you are responsible and always take initiative, give him some examples. Preparing for an interview is a rehearsal just like anything else you may be trying to achieve.

Another helpful hint, after completing a interview, is to send a follow up thank you note or letter right away in the mail. Why? Because if there were a few candidates that they could not decide on and your thank you card comes in the mail, it could be the critical difference which makes you look special. In addition, in the card or letter you can add something else you may have forgotten to mention in the interview.

20 Common Interview Questions

These are 20 commonly asked interview questions

The employer wants to find out:
- Personal Information about you.
- What you can offer the company.
- What you know about the job.

1. Tell me a little about yourself.
2. What are your strengths?
3. What are your weaknesses?
4. What did you like best/least about previous jobs you have held?
5. What duties did you perform on your last job?
6. Tell me what you think good customer service is.
7. Tell me about a time when you had to deal with an angry person and how you handled the situation.
8. Why should we hire you for this job?
9. Why are you interested in working for our company?
10. Have you ever been a member of a team when someone wasn't doing their part? What did you do or say?
11. Do you prefer working alone or as a member of a team?
12. Tell me about a time when you had a lot of work to do within a short time and how you completed it in a timely manner.
13. Tell me about a time when a co-worker criticized your work. How did you react?
14. Tell me about the last time you had a problem or complaint on your job. How did you handle it?
15. What salary are you looking for?
16. Why should I hire you?
17. Where do you see yourself in five years?
18. What qualities do you look for in a supervisor?
19. Can you get recommendations? What will your references say about you?
20. Do you have any questions for me?

Questions You May Want To Ask

TWO WAY PROCESS: A good interview is a two-way process. It is as much an opportunity for you to learn about the potential job and organization as it is for a prospective new supervisor to find out about you. You should, therefore, feel free to ask questions as well.

Always ask a question that shows interest and enthusiasm for the job.

COMMON QUESTIONS: Some questions you may want to consider asking are as follows:

- Can you describe a typical day in this job?
- What are the expectations for this position?
- How will my performance be evaluated for this job?
- What type of person would be best suited for this position?
- Are there special requirements for this job; i.e., travel, overtime?
- How do you see my skills and experience fitting with the job?
- What are the next steps in this interviewing process?
- Do you have a probation period?
- Are there opportunities for advancement
- What is the dress code?
- When do you anticipate making your decision?

Personal Strengths

Good worker traits you can offer to an Employer:

Use to sell yourself in interviews or add a few to your Resumé.

Able to meet deadlines
Able to prioritize
Able to work under pressure
Able to work well unsupervised
Assertive , Bilingual
Can work independently
Committed
Conscientious
Considerate
Creative
Dedicated
Delegate
Dependable
Detail oriented
Diligent
Disciplined
Eager to Learn
Enthusiastic
Facilitator
Fast learner
Flexible
Follow safety rules
Friendly, Focused
Goal oriented
Good communication skills
Good listening skills

Good with numbers
Honest
Knowledgeable
Leader, Loyal
Meticulous
Mechanically Inclined
Multi-task oriented
Neat, Organized
Patient
Persistent
Planner
Positive
Productive, Resourceful
Punctual, Problem Solver
Responsible
Self-motivated
Sense of humor
Strong managerial skills
Take initiative
Take on challenges
Team player
Time management skills
Verbal & Written Skills
Willing to do extra work to
gain valuable experience
Willing to follow directions

If You're Offered the Job

Before you accept, evaluate the position carefully in terms of:

- Job Responsibility
- Working Hours
- Pace of Work
- Advancement opportunities
- Salary range
- Benefits
- Job Location

- Transportation requirements- is public transport available or do you need a car?
- Working Conditions
- Future possibilities- what could the job lead to?

If you accept, you may want to write a confirming note (even if you've accepted verbally.) Make sure to confirm your starting date & time. Also know what the dress code is, do not assume anything.

How to Keep Your Job

Be Punctual

Always be on time or early, call the employer if you will not be there or if you are late. Be responsible & show good work ethics. Especially if you want to be promoted.

Show Initiative

Always be ready to find things to do or ask what else you can do, look busy & always go the extra mile.

Be Aware of Safety Rules

Employers do not want to keep people who have accidents or who do not follow the safety rules. It is costly and dangerous to others.

Be a Team player

Assist others; people depend on one another in work situations. Be able to work in a group, be goal oriented, have creative ideas, integrity and leadership skills. Good communication is also essential. There is No "I" in Team!

Be Enthusiastic

Always act like you enjoy your job, when you do, you become a more productive worker. Make sure to smile & focus on the positive.

Be Conscientious

Learn to be diligent, focused, avoid gossip, dress appropriately, show appreciation for others. Do not come to work under the influence. Always use good judgment.

Be Respectful

If you do not like your job, look for something else on your days off. Make sue to always give two weeks notice &

give them a letter of resignation. In addition, ask for a letter of reference. Leave things in an organized manner for someone else.

Be Inquisitive

Take courses. Improve your methods. Make every effort to grow with your organization.

"People Acting Together as a Group Can Accomplish Things. Which No Individual Acting Alone Could Ever Hope to Bring About."
- Franklin Delano Roosevelt

If the job is not right for you—do not despair. Start your job search again. Consider additional training. Move on up! In the meantime, make the most of your present job. It will mean good references, on-the job experience and a chance to grow.

Example Letter of Resignation

Date:

Ms. Robin Rask
Manager
Diamond's Restaurant
7777 Diamond Drive
Victorville, CA 92393

Dear Ms. Rask:

Please accept my resignation from my job as a cashier. My last day of work will be September 2005. I will be accepting a position with more work hours.

I appreciate the wonderful experience and training I have had at Diamond's Restaurant. I have learned many valuable job skill tools while working with you. I will be more than happy to train my replacement. Thank you for accepting my resignation.

Sincerely,

MaryAnn Needy

MaryAnn Needy

Why People May Not Get Hired

Positive Reasons:

1. Too many applicants.
2. A former employee changed his or her mind and decided not to leave.
3. Your skills are more than what is needed for the position.
4. They cannot pay you what you are making now.
5. They are looking for more experience.
6. They are only accepting applications for a future need.
7. Lack of experience on part of interviewer.
8. They are only trying to fill a temporary position.

Negative Reasons:

1. Poor personal appearance.
2. Overbearing-overaggressive (know- it- all) attitude.
3. Inability to express yourself clearly, poor voice, poor grammar.
4. Lack of planning for career, no purpose or goals.
5. Lack of interest and enthusiasm, passive, indifferent.
6. Lack of confidence and poise, nervousness, ill at ease.
7. Overemphasis on salary, interest only in dollar offer.
8. Poor grades, just did well enough to pass.
9. Unwilling to start at entry level; expects too much too soon.
10. Makes excuses for past work record.
11. Fails to make eye contact with the interviewer.
12. Limp, fishy handshake.
13. Sloppy application.
14. Wants only temporary position.
15. Late to interview without a valid excuse.
16. Applicant knows nothing about the company.
17. Failure to express appreciation for interviewer's time.
18. Gives indefinite responses to questions.

Printed by permission, Partners & Education/Youth Programs/Poway Unified School District

Chapter Ten

PORTFOLIOS

STEP SEVEN / Portfolios

A portfolio is a highly effective tool to assist you in obtaining employment. When you go on interviews, you should take a portfolio with you to let the employer see that you may have something to share.

A portfolio is simply putting a notebook together of your accomplishments. You may want to purchase some sheet protectors to put your documents in such as your resum'e, your certificates, your recommendation letters, references and anything else that is important.

You may want to get reference letters from teachers, past employers etc. Try to get them on company letterhead and they must be typed. The recommendation letters basically say how wonderful you are and that they would recommend you for a job. Everyone should have at least two to three in their portfolio. If you have never worked before you can get one from someone you babysat for, it can be the pastor of a church, teacher or a coach. Anyone other then family members or friends that can say good things about you.

Alternatively, you can bring samples of your work. You can put a portfolio together for the specific job you want.

For instance if you are trying to get a job as a graphic artist or architect, you will want to demonstrate and show off your work or bring samples. You may not have much to put in your portfolio at the beginning, the point is just to get started and keep adding to it.

There is a separate sheet with a list of ideas included.

It has been said, "There is no traffic in the extra mile and always give people more than they expect."

Work Portfolios

May Include:

- Drawings
- Actual product samples small enough
  to be brought into the interview
- Paper samples of work
- Photographs that document work with descriptions
  of planning and progress to completion.

Materials to include in your portfolio:

Sample of Completed Job Application
Resumé
Letters of Recommendation
Certificates/ Awards
References with Addresses and Phone Numbers
Copy of High School Diploma
Colleges, Private Schools
Transcripts only if proud
List of Elective Subjects with Course Descriptions
Report Cards for H.S. students with 3.0 or better
List of Paid Work Experience
List of Unpaid Work Experience and Volunteer Work
Vocational Training/ Internships & Externships
R.O.P. Classes
Job Corps, California Conservation Corp, Armed Services
J.T.P.A./ W.I.A./ Workability, T.P.P.
Adult Supported Employment Programs
Pictures of Accomplishments/ Things You Have Done/ Clubs
Organizations/ Outside Activities/ Community Service
Test Results/ Assessments
Examples of How You Use Teamwork
Other

Letters of Recommendation

Your portfolio should include letter(s) of recommendation. You should ask people who know you, your personality, attitude, skills, etc., to provide letters of recommendation. These individuals may be from your list of personal references, current or past employers, teachers, counselors, or your minister. Letters of recommendation cannot be from relatives or friends.

Instructions:

❑ Letters must be typed. (If handwritten, type it and have the writer sign it).

❑ The letter should be addressed "To Whom It May Concern".

❑ The letter should be written to a prospective future employer recommending you for a job because of your skills, habits, personality, and other attributes known by the letter writer.

A Sample Letter Of Recommendation Is Shown Below:

To Whom It May Concern:

I am writing this letter on behalf of Shauna Smith. Shauna worked for me during the summer of 2005 at my Real Estate Office. She was a great help in reorganizing our files, answering phones, typing, and giving assistance to customers. Shauna has the ability to use computers and knows some common software programs. She works hard and is very reliable.

I believe Shauna would be an excellent employee and I highly recommend her to future employers. She will be an asset to any business that hires her. Please feel free to give me a call at 955-0000 if I may be of assistance or answer any questions about Shauna.

Sincerely,

Robin Rask

Robin Rask

Chapter Eleven

ATTITUDE & SELF-ESTEEM

STEP EIGHT / Attitude & Self-Esteem

I believe having a positive attitude and being motivated are two essential elements for finding a job and anything else for that matter. If you are not motivated to look for a job, what will motivate you to go to work when you have one? Maybe money! A lot of people obtain a job and turn around and loose it shortly after. Once you have a job you will have to work on your work ethics to keep it. Many people come to me and say, "Miss Rask, I need a job." When I remind them of the steps they need to take to find a job, they do not want to do it because it is too much work. They just want me to say sure you can start on Monday at 9:00 at XYZ Company.

I do not know what the problem is with today's society, I think some have it too good and are too spoiled. I did not have a computer or cell phone when I was going to High School and I was raised differently. Back then people seemed to have values and worked hard for what they wanted, it should be no different today. Some people just want everything handed to them. I know when people spoil their kids at a young age and they get everything they want, they do not appreciate it down the road.

There are many people who seem to have very low self-esteem or are depressed for various reasons. They may have been abused in a variety of ways or talked down upon. If someone constantly tells you that you are no good, it may give you low self-esteem in a hurry. No matter the reason, if you have poor self-esteem then that is something you may want to work on. Especially, if you plan on seeking employment and going through job interviews. As you may recall, the number one question in an interview is usually, "tell me about yourself." Therefore, you will need to learn to say positive things about yourself. Let me give you a few suggestions on how to work on your self-esteem which will improve your attitude and give you self-confidence. You can use the mirror concept just like you would prepare for the interview.

* Affirmations & Changes, write down all the positive things about yourself that you can think of. Then start remembering some and say them every day. For example, when you look in the mirror every morning start confessing out of your mouth that you are kind, beautiful, energetic, caring, responsible, eager to learn, organized, and whatever else applies to you. It takes 21-30 days to make or break a habit. If you say positive things about yourself every morning eventually, you will become what you say and believe. Do not say anything negative about yourself no matter how you may be feeling. If you always say, "I am too fat and can not loose weight" then you probably wont. You are talking yourself into what you say. This works in the negative and in the positive. There is power in thoughts and words. If you want to make changes, you need to make a decision on the inside first to do so. Write down the things you want to change and then take baby steps towards your goals. Change comes from being diligent; if you do not change your way of thinking, you won't change your life.

* Compliments & Put downs: When someone pays you a compliment, such as, " I like your new hair style," do not say anything negative especially if you do not like it. Just simply say, "Thank you" and go on. When someone puts you down or says something hurtful, just take it with a grain of salt, shake it off, smile, and go on. If it is too hard to take, just say to yourself "God help me to stay calm with a good attitude."

* Relationships: It has been said, "You are whom you hang out with." If you hang out with people who are always complaining, that will affect you. If you hang around people who smoke, you may be tempted to smoke, etc. Find people you can trust and can help you and always try to hang around people who are positive and have goals.

* Accepting Yourself: We are not all born beautiful, skinny, rich, educated and talented. Therefore, we sometimes envy those who are. We all have to play the cards we were dealt and be thankful we even have a chance to be in the game and on this earth. God made us all in his own image and thinks we are all beautiful. He designed each of us differently with different looks, skills, and talents. He put special gifts into each of us, we have to figure out what those gifts are and fulfill our destiny.

There will always be someone who is prettier, skinnier, smarter, talented and has more than you. That is just life. God also intended for all of us to prosper and be in good health. So, like yourself for whom you are and do the best you can with what you have. You are a classic original; there is no one else like you.

"Always be a first rate version of yourself instead of a second rate version of somebody else."
-Judy Garland

"It is not what you've got, it's what you use that makes a difference."
-Zig Ziggler

Renewing your Mind with Affirmations for Positive Change

Affirmations are positive, they start with "I am, I have or I will"

I am living in a beautiful house overlooking the ocean.

Say what you are, what you want, and where you want to be as if it already is! Get a picture of what you want to do or obtain, see yourself doing it and with it. Your life will follow your thoughts. We draw in what we constantly think about. When you look in the mirror every day say positive confessions about yourself. Become what you believe.

Repeat your affirmations daily! *

There are no age limits in when you can transform your life. Change is possible at any time and is essential if you want to grow.

Power in Thoughts and Words

- We have to change our thinking if we want to renew our minds.
- Everything we do starts with a decision.
- Nothing happens on the outside till it starts on the inside first.
- We must possess a strong desire to change
- Expect to succeed
- Expect the best
- Start expecting big things (GOD is a big GOD)

- Believe for more
- Dream Big Dreams
- Hang around dreamers
- Think before you speak
- Defend your mind against old thoughts
- Don't waste any more time on things that are over
- Avoid negative thoughts and words, replace with positive
- Don't get stuck in the same rut
- Don't be satisfied with where you are.
- Be selective of what you expose yourself to
- If you keep doing what you have always done, you will get what you always got.
- Once you find your purpose in life, you are driven by it.
- Know what produces good fruit in your life
- We have the power to capture every thought
- Change comes from being diligent
- Consistency is the key to all victory

Trials and Challenges

- Your challenges can be your greatest assets
- Your trial is a test of your character
- Sometimes trials come in groups
- Quit focusing on your problems
- When you get into a trial say, "This is one of those times when my emotions are being tried. I am going to trust God and learn to control them." Try to look at your problem as an opportunity to work out for your good. Stay happy in the middle of your circumstances as difficult as it may be. Trials bring out patience.
- Patience is not just putting up with; it is consistently and constantly remaining the same and long suffering. *

- Life is 10% of what happens to you and 90% of how we react to it.
- Say " I can do all things I need to do"
- Constantly put on a fresh attitude.
- If you don't like the circle you are standing in, then step out of it
- Look past where you are and look towards your future.
- No time with God equals failure
- Be a blessing everywhere you go
- If you want more, give away some of what you have
- Life is all about sewing and reaping, whatever you sew, you will eventually reap.
- Sew a smile you will reap a smile
- Sew kindness you will reap kindness
- Sew sparingly you will reap sparingly, sew generously you will reap generously*
- Be a prisoner of hope, stir yourself up
- Say "Today is my receiving day, something good is going to happen to me"

** PRAY-WAIT-BELIEVE-EXPECT

**EXPECT CHANGE-EVERYTHING IS SUBJECT TO CHANGE!!

Self-Esteem

Appreciating my own worth and importance and having the character to be accountable for myself and to act responsible for others!!!

-Anonymous

CHAPTER TWELVE

TIME MANAGEMENT

STEP NINE / Time Management

Time is a precious commodity! Time management has little to do with managing your time; it is all about learning to manage yourself more effectively. Everyone has 24 hours in a day and seven days in a week! How you spend, your time is up to you. Most people say, "I am too busy or I do not have time!" Everyone is busy doing something or busy doing nothing.

We all make our own schedules; we need to make time for what is important. Get up earlier, go to bed later, do the important things first then you can have fun. Many people procrastinate, when you know you need to do something, do it now, and be done with it. You may also have to learn to say no to some things or to your friends. If you have too much on your plate then learn to delegate, or hire someone to help you with your chores etc. Put your money where your time is! If you learn to start using your time more wisely and effectively, you will be surprised how much time, you have left to do the extras and have fun too.

In order to have good time management skills it is essential that you make good use of your time. You need to be organized, focused, have discipline and learn to set priorities.

I am including a one-week time management chart. Write down everything you do for a week in ½ hour and 1 hour increments. At the end of each day, total the hours that you think you wasted or were unproductive. Then add the total for the week. It will be interesting to see how you spend your 168 hours a week. We all make time for what we want to do.

If you want more information on this topic, please read some Time Management Books. Or look for my future book on Self Management to Time Management.

> **"What lies behind us and what lies before us are
> tiny matters compared to what lies within us."**
> *–Oliver Wendell Holmes*

> **"I have time for whatever I need to make time for."**
> *-Robin L. Rask*

⏱ TIME MANAGEMENT ⏱

	Sunday	Monday	Tuesday	Wednesday	Thursday	Friday	Saturday
12:00am							
12:30am							
1:00pm							
1:30pm							
2:00pm							
2:30pm							
3:00pm							
3:30pm							
4:00pm							
4:30pm							
5:00pm							
5:30pm							

6:00pm							
6:30pm							
7:00pm							
7:30pm							
8:00pm							
8:30pm							
9:00pm							
9:30pm							
10:00pm							
10:30pm							
11:00pm							
11:30pm							
Wasted PM Hours							
Total Wasted Hours							

⏱ TIME MANAGEMENT ⏱

	Sunday	Monday	Tuesday	Wednesday	Thursday	Friday	Saturday
12:00pm							
12:30pm							
1:00am							
1:30am							
2:00am							
2:30am							
3:00am							
3:30am							
4:00am							
4:30am							
5:00am							
5:30am							

6:00am								
6:30am								
7:00am								
7:30am								
8:00am								
8:30am								
9:00am								
9:30am								
10:00am								
10:30am								
11:00am								
11:30am								
Wasted PM Hours								
Total Wasted Hours								

Time Management

Everyone has **24** hours in a day and **7** days in a week! How you spend your time is up to you. In order to have good time management skills it is essential that you make good use of your time and learn to set priorities.

Everyone is busy doing something or busy doing nothing. People always say, "I am too busy" or "I don't have time." Truly, we all make time for what we want to do or not!

**If you want to have great time management skills
you need to be organized, focused, disciplined
and learn to manage your self not your time!**

Thomas Edison said, "There is time for everything"

14 Steps To Success

BE CONFIDENT – Successful people believe in themselves. They know their actions make a difference in their lives and the lives of others. They work at trusting themselves and others.

BE RESPONSIBLE – Successful people choose to respond with appropriate behavior and accept the consequences of their actions. They take credit for their success and learn from their mistakes.

BE HERE – Successful people go to work regularly. Once there, they are both physically and mentally present.

BE PROMPT – Successful people are always prompt. They get to where they are going on time. Others are counting on them to be on time.

BE FRIENDLY – Successful people accept the differences of others. They build friendships by helping one another rather than hurting each other. Unsuccessful people destroy by acting or speaking out in violence.

BE POLITE – Successful people show courtesy. They acknowledge the fact that other people have helped them become successful. With that in mind, they have respect for others. For instance, politely waiting their turn.

BE PREPARED – Successful people always come prepared with their materials when expected. They keep their tools and supplies in good condition. To be prepared, a successful person must always plan ahead.

BE A LISTENER – Successful people listen to instructions and follow directions. Since they listen to what others need, they can cooperate to achieve success.

BE A WORKER – Successful people keep working. They spend their time on the things that will generate production and earnings. They will keep focused even when others get off track.

BE A TOUGH WORKER – Successful people keep trying. They keep trying towards their goals even when things get difficult.

BE A RISK TAKER – Successful people have courage and are willing to run the risk of failure. They know that sooner or later they will reach their goals if they keep trying.

BE A GOAL SETTER – Successful people plan for the future. They use goals as a personal road map to guide them where they want to go. By setting goals, people are able to realize their dreams.

ALWAYS BE POSITIVE – Be aware of a negative attitude in yourself and others. You should avoid those with a negative attitude.

REMEMBER – When you blame somebody else for your troubles, you have automatically given him or her power.

Printed by permission

"The longer I live, the more I realize the impact of attitude on life. Attitude to me is more important than facts, more important than the past, than education, than money, than circumstances, than failures, than success, than whatever people think, say, or do. It is more important than appearance, talent, or skill. It will make or break a company or a home. The remarkable thing is that we have a choice every day regarding the attitude we will embrace for that day. We cannot change the inevitable. The only thing we can do is play on the one string we have, and that is our attitude. I am convinced that life is 10% what happens to me and 90% how I react to it. And so it is with you. We are in charge of our lives."

Charles Swindoll

Robin's Simple Recipe For Finding a Job!!

Apply where you want to work and keep on going back and keep on going back to let them know you are interested in working there. Always dress to interview when you apply for a job and always go alone. Fill out your application neatly and completely, if something does not apply to you write N/A. Always use black or blue pen, take white out with you or an erasable pen. You may attach a resumé to your application or make sure to bring one to your interview.

When you turn in your application ask for the manager so that you can introduce yourself. Shake their hand, smile and show enthusiasm. Say, "Nice to meet you. I just wanted to give you my application and let you know that I am interested in working here." That is all you have to say. When you leave write down where you went, the date, the managers name and what they said. Keep a log sheet of everywhere you go. When you go back to do your weekly or bi-weekly follow up, you will know who to ask for. If they tell you to come back on a certain day or time, make sure that you do. If they tell you to call on Tuesday at 4:00 and you don't, then that tells the employer that you do not want the job.

The more places that you go to apply and follow up on, the sooner you will get hired. Many times you will be interviewed on the spot, so be prepared. The number one question that is asked in interviews is "Tell me about yourself," so you need to be ready to talk about yourself. Let them know what your strengths are, what kind of person you are and how you can fit in with their company. Work on your personal attributes, we all have them. Example: Look in the mirror every morning and start talking to yourself. Say whatever applies to you such as, "I am a team player, organized, creative, fast learner, responsible, always take initiative and have great time management skills." Making personal confessions of your attributes will make you a more positive person and you will be able to sell yourself better in an interview. It will also help you to have a portfolio to bring with you to your interview.

Some of the things to put in your portfolio are:

Resumé, References, Recommendation letters
Certificates, awards, report cards, transcripts
Vocational trainings, internships, R.O.P classes, pictures of accomplishments
Outside activities, clubs, community service, etc.

You don't have a second chance to make a first impression!

Make sure you stay persistent and follow up!

If you are looking for a job and can't find one, you either don't know how to effectively search for a job or you are not motivated.

Remember to network, use all your resources and attend Job Fairs. There are many services available that help people get jobs.

There is someone hiring everyday!

Good Luck! R.L.R.

ABOUT THE AUTHOR

Robin has been an Employment Specialist over 17 years. It was not a career she originally chose. She believes it is a gift from God as part of her purpose in life. When Robin was in School there were no R.O.P. programs or people teaching you how to obtain jobs or even putting you to work to receive job training. Or at least she did not know about them. People today are so fortunate to have so many wonderful beneficial programs and resources available to them. Robin had to learn everything the hard way when it came to finding a job.

When she did her first Resumé, which was after High School it was three pages long, which included references. Her Resumé was also full of I's. I did this and I did that. How embarrassing and humiliating that was especially since this was not taught when she went to school. She put personal information on her Resumé that did not belong. When she filled out applications and it asked for salary desired she put $1200 a month. That was back when minimum wage was $3.25. Employers must have fallen out of their chairs laughing when they saw that. By the way, minimum wage was at $3.25 & 4.25 for a very long time.

After trial and errors, she quickly learned what worked and what did not. She also began researching and speaking with professionals. It was by the grace of God she was hired back then. One thing she always did right was to Dress to Impress, which her Mom, Bernadette

Murphy Neal taught her at a very early age. Never leave the house unless you look good, no matter where you go; even if it is just to the store. You never know you may meet your special someone in the produce department! She did once, but he was not the right person. In other words, do not go to the store or leave your home in curlers.

The first job Robin had was in a grocery store and she was referred for that. The only prior experience she had then was childcare and doing yard work for neighbors. Some times, it is whom you know not what you know. Robin has a great deal of gratitude for her parents teaching her good work ethics, though when she was younger often resented it. When her friends were out having fun, Robin was cleaning house, preparing meals and doing yard work. That is still true today! When her son David was a baby, she taught him to pick up his toys before he could walk because he never crawled. So he has also learned good work habits ever since and how to be responsible now as an adult. He will then pass this on to his kids and so on and so on, that is how it should work.

This is part of the value system the world is lacking today. Good values and work ethics are supposed to be taught at home at an early age. Our society and generation would be so much different today. Hopefully this will change because our kids today and our grand kids will be our future educators and presidents tomorrow.

Robin has been teaching people how to find a job for so many years that she wanted to put her teachings into a book for all job seekers to read and apply. When Robin teaches workshops on how to obtain employment she does not sugar coat anything. She is brief and to the point. She knows what Employers are looking for. Her son, David followed her simple steps and he now obtains employment every time. Along with many others who take and seek her advice.

Robin has worked two jobs plus most of her life, which takes a great deal of time management skills, focus and discipline. It is not always about the money it is about making a difference in the world and in people's lives. So, some of her jobs are volunteer. Which can look great on your Resumés?

Robin remembers saying to herself as a teenager when she retires she will write a book. Obviously, God instructed her to do it now. Which must be part of the reason that Robin is a now person. Her work ethics are, when something needs to be done, do it immediately instead of procrastinating.

In her spare time, she enjoys working in the yard for therapy. She enjoys the Beach, water sports, music, C.C., Tennis, traveling, reading, taking pictures, assisting others in need and she tries to be a blessing whenever and wherever she goes.

Robin does not have letters in front of her name or a PHD, however she does have a Professional High School Diploma, Vocational Credential in Personnel Administration and is Past Having Doubt. Finding a job is all about learning to sell yourself and marketing yourself.

www.ingramcontent.com/pod-product-compliance
Lightning Source LLC
Chambersburg PA
CBHW022025170526
45157CB00003B/1349